W9-BUR-247

SOUTH SHORE BRANCH
2505 EAST 73rd STREET
CHICAGO ILLINOIS 60649

S is for Shamrock

An Ireland Alphabet

Written by Eve Bunting and Illustrated by Matt Faulkner

To all my Irish friends and relatives.

EVE

For my pal, Ralph Masiello, a great father, friend, and artist!

MATT

Sleeping Bear Press™
310 North Main Street, Suite 300
Chelsea, MI 48118
www.sleepingbearpress.com

© 2007 Thomson Gale, a part of the Thomson Corporation.

Thomson, Star Logo and Sleeping Bear Press are trademarks
and Gale is a registered trademark used herein under license.

Printed and bound in Canada.

First Edition

10 9 8 7 6 5 4 3 2 1

Library of Congress Cataloging-in-Publication Data

Bunting, Eve, 1928-
S is for shamrock : an Ireland alphabet / written by Eve Bunting ;
illustrated by Matt Faulkner.
p. cm.
Summary: "From A to Z, Ireland is presented in poetry, prose, and illustrations.
Topics include Blarney Stone, Finn McCool, fairy rings, and shamrocks."
—Provided by publisher.
ISBN 13: 978-1-58536-290-5
ISBN 10: 1-58536-290-5
1. Ireland—Social life and customs—Juvenile literature. 2. Northern Ireland—
Social life and customs—Juvenile literature. 3. Ireland—History—Juvenile literature.
4. Northern Ireland—History—Juvenile literature. I. Faulkner, Matt, ill. II. Title.
DA925.B85 2007
941.5—dc22   2006026000

Scotland
(U.K.)

Northern Ireland
(U.K.)

*Irish
Sea*

Dublin ★

*North
Atlantic
Ocean*

Ireland

The small island of Ireland has been invaded by many countries.

Around 400 BC Celtic tribes came from the European mainland bringing with them the Gaelic language, which is still spoken in parts of Ireland today.

Then from Denmark and Norway came the Norsemen in their longships. They began as raiders, pillaging the country, but eventually established communities such as Cork and Dublin.

The Anglo-Norman invaders came around 1160. Soon, like the Norsemen before them, the Normans, too, intermarried, adopted the Irish language, and lost their loyalty to England. However, England continued to control Ireland, and still controls a part of it.

Throughout all these invasions the Irish have never accepted a foreign government and fight against it still. Today, patriots everywhere raise their voices in the toast "Erin go Bragh"—Ireland Forever.

A is for Ancient Ireland

This ancient land was pillaged, raided.
Many times it was invaded,
taken over, occupied.
In spite of all it still survived.

"Blarney" is a word that means talking so sweetly and persuasively and believably that you can charm your way out of any situation. In Ireland it's called "having the gift of the gab" and a lot of Irish seem to come by it naturally.

Talking "blarney" can also mean talking foolishly, or in an exaggerated way. But "blarney" is charming and it is laughed at and admired.

The Blarney Stone is set in the 18-foot (5.4 meter)-thick wall of Blarney Castle in the Irish village of Blarney. It's said that if you kiss the stone the gift of gab will be yours. The problem is, it's not that easy to reach it. You have to lie on your back and bend back and down, down, holding on to an iron bar, or have someone else hold your feet.

Does it work? Will you now have the gift of the gab? Or is the whole thing just a load of—blarney?

B b

B is for Blarney Stone

When you kiss the Blarney stone
please be sure you're not alone.
You have to hang with your head down,
upside down in Blarney town.

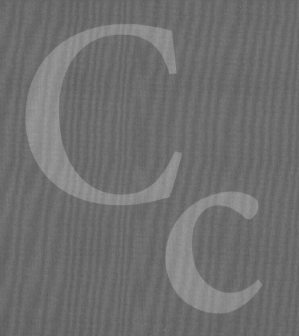

Claddagh is a fishing village near Galway town in Ireland. Richard Joyce, a Galway man, was taken from Ireland as a slave and sold to a Turkish goldsmith who taught him to work with gold and silver. The goldsmith taught him well.

In 1689 when Joyce was released from slavery, he went home and set up shop in Claddagh. The rings he made showed two hands holding a heart with a crown floating above. The hands represented friendship, the crown loyalty, and the heart love.

A Claddagh ring became a family treasure, passed down from generation to generation. During the years of the Great Famine (1845–1850) many treasured rings were sold to buy passage out of the horror that Ireland had become.

Claddagh rings are still found anywhere there are Irish with a feel for tradition. In some parts of Ireland it is so important to use a Claddagh ring in the wedding ceremony that a poor bridegroom will rent one for the occasion.

C is for the Claddagh ring

The Claddagh ring has two clasped hands,
a heart between, a crown above.
It's worn in friendship, or perhaps
a token of forever love.

D is for Dublin

The river Liffey glides along
singing its old river song
of saints and scholars,
joy and pain,
of martyrs dead, but not in vain.

Dublin is the capital and the largest city of the Republic of Ireland. It has three cathedrals and a castle that was originally a prison. Decapitated heads were once displayed on poles outside its walls.

Dublin has Trinity College, home to famous scholars and writers. It has wide, tree-lined streets and stately Georgian houses with doors so wildly colorful, so unexpected, that they have their own "Dublin Doors" poster sold worldwide. Dublin has the river Liffey with twelve bridges reaching over it. One is "The Ha'penny Bridge," because a ha'penny was the sum you once had to pay to walk across it.

Dublin was originally a small, walled village founded by Norsemen in the ninth century. Now it is a city with close to a million people. Still, Leon Uris, the novelist, once described it as "an intimate city where everyone knows everyone and no one dresses very well!"

That's Dublin!

Dd

E is for Ellis Island

To Ellis Island they all came:
"Where did you come from?"
"What's your name?"
"Irish, Russian, Jew, and Finn,
America will let you in."

Ellis Island is in New York harbor. From 1892 to 1924, it was used as a reception center for immigrants coming to the United States.

Annie Moore was a red-haired Irish girl from County Cork, going to America with her two younger brothers to be reunited with their parents. It was New Year's Day, 1892, when their ship docked. It was also Annie's fifteenth birthday. She was first in line to step ashore when a bearded Russian immigrant tried to take her place. An Irishman pulled him back. "Ladies first," he said, and little Annie Moore became the first immigrant ever to step ashore on Ellis Island.

There is a statue of Annie at the Ellis Island Immigration Museum and another in the harbor at Cobh in County Cork. The two statues symbolize not only the 500,000 Irish who passed through Ellis Island, but all the immigrants who left their homes for America.

F f

F is for Fairy Rings

You can find a fairy ring
     where fairies meet to dance and sing.
Is there a fairy town below
     where only fairy people go?

Fairy rings are round earth walls found in fields all over Ireland. Built from 500 to 1100, they were really ringforts made to protect homes and families. They have lasted all these years because it is believed that fairies live in and under them.

There are more than 40,000 fairy rings in Ireland, which makes them the most numerous of old Irish monuments.

The enchanted rings are supposed to open on Halloween. Fairy music drifts from them—music so beautiful that it entices anyone who hears it to leave home and family and "be off with the fairies." Better keep your distance or the fairies may "make away" with you, and you'll never be content to live among humans again.

G is for the Giant's Causeway

The Irish giant, Finn McCool,
never went a day to school.
But he was big, and strong, and smart.
This causeway was for his sweetheart.

The Giant's Causeway marches into the Irish Sea between Ireland and Scotland. It is made of basalt stones shaped like hexagonal columns, set so close together that the line of them looks like a road. Geologists say the columns were caused by volcanic action.

Not at all, say the Irish.

The Giant's Causeway was the work of Finn McCool, Ireland's favorite giant. When he fell in love with a lady giant on Staffa, an island in the Hebrides, Finn built this causeway to bring her comfortably back to Ulster. A giant-sized rowboat might have worked for the two of them, but Finn was a giant who liked to make a statement. And his statement still stands, strange and beautiful along the northern coast of Ireland at the place where the land ends.

G g

H is for Hedge Schools

Sitting here beneath the sky,
no roof above to keep me dry.
"Will you teach me how to read?
Please, teacher, that is all I need."

The English Penal Laws of the eighteenth century forbade Catholics to attend Catholic worship, to purchase land, to own a horse of greater value than five pounds, or to receive an education. Secret hedge schools sprang up. They were so called because the teacher taught illegally and dangerously under a hedge or in a barn if the weather was bad. A student would be posted on a hilltop to warn of approaching British soldiers.

The schoolmasters taught reading, writing, arithmetic, and sometimes Latin. They educated the children of Ireland.

"To these hedge schoolmasters who at the cost of their happiness and risk of their lives fed the little flame of knowledge among the hills and glens of Ireland ... Ireland can never repay her debt."
(Seamus McManus: *The Story of the Irish Race.*)

The Irish wolfhound is the tallest of all dogs. If it stands on its back legs it measures more than six feet in height. Bred in Ireland to hunt wolves and giant elk, it could be owned only by kings and noblemen. Strong and courageous, the hounds rode with their kings into battle. So revered is the wolfhound that its image has been used on famous Irish glassware, on an Irish coin, and on a postage stamp. So treasured is it that in the seventeenth century, by law, it could not be taken out of Ireland. That law no longer applies.

In the Gettysburg National Battlefield in Pennsylvania there is a stone effigy of an Irish wolfhound lying at the base of a Celtic cross. It commemorates the soldiers of the Irish Brigade who died, far from home, in the American Civil War.

I i

I is for Irish wolfhound

The wolfhound is a noble dog.
    He'll seldom gallop, prance, or jog,
but strides along with stately grace
    befitting his exalted place!

J is for Journey

The ship is waiting at the quay.
I'm crying and it's hard to see.
I try to smile. I wave my hand.
Goodbye, goodbye, my Ireland.

N is for Nature

The Mountains of Mourne, the Vale of Tralee,
the green hills of Antrim, the dark Irish Sea.
The patchwork of fields stretching mile after mile,
a "terrible beauty," the Emerald Isle.

N n

Ireland is a small island, less than four hundred miles (644 km) from north to south, and less than two hundred miles (322 km) from east to west. The climate is temperate, which means it's seldom too hot or too cold. But it does rain a lot!

It is and always has been a country of small farms. Potatoes are grown, and oats and hay to feed the livestock that provide milk and butter and cheese, some of it for export.

Those who live there and those who visit agree—Ireland is a beautiful country. There's a softness to the emerald green fields, divided here and there by smooth, stone walls. The mountains that are little more than high hills seem to be forever misty. Sheep, sometimes marked with daubs of bright paint to indicate their owners, graze on their hillsides.

Ireland has been serenaded in poetry and literature, often longingly by those who have left it.

"Maybe someday I'll go back to Ireland."

Maybe.

Maybe someday.

The Irish love to trace their family trees.

If your name starts with O or O' it usually means you are "the descendant of" or "grandson of" an ancient king or chieftain, many centuries ago.

The O'Donnells, for instance, were one of the grandest families in Ireland, descended from Niall of the Nine Hostages. O'Toole comes from the tenth-century King of Leinster. If you are an O'Malley, your great, great grandmother, way back, could have been Grace O'Malley, the Pirate Queen of Mayo, who was captured several times and just escaped the gallows. In her old age she was so famous that she visited Queen Elizabeth I in London as "a princess and an equal."

O is for O'

O'Neill, OBrien, and O'Dea,
O'Rourke, O'Connor, and O'Shea—
Irish names that start with O'
passed down from kinfolk long ago.

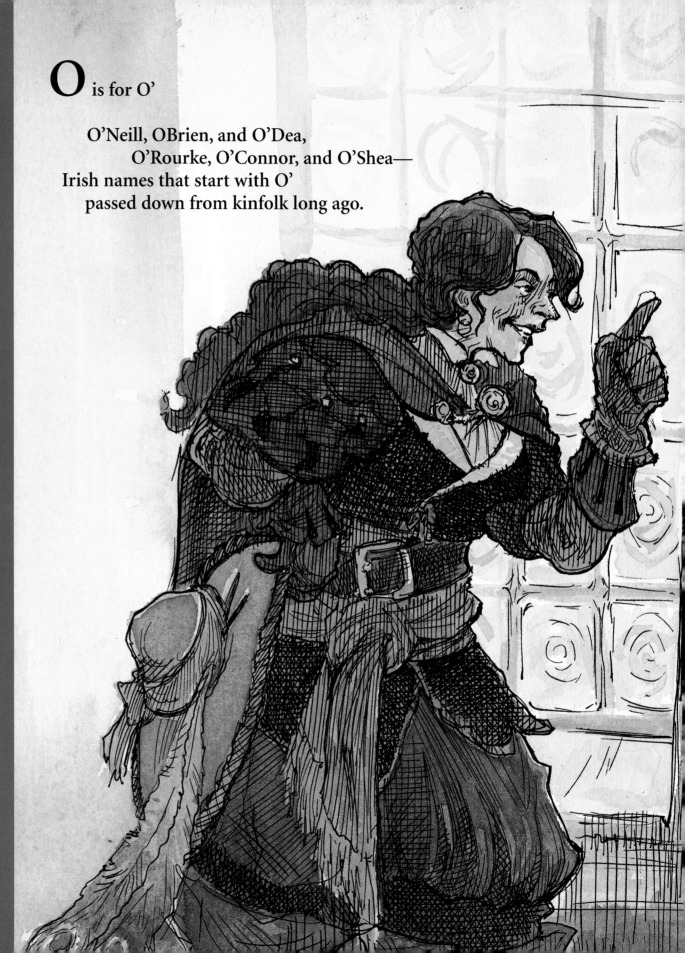

P p

P is for St. Patrick

St. Patrick taught the fish to jump.
He drove the snakes away.
It seems the whole world honors him
on each St. Patrick's Day!

St. Patrick's name wasn't Patrick. He wasn't born in Ireland and in the beginning he wasn't even a saint.

His name was Maewyn, born in Wales or perhaps France, around 385. Snatched from his father's home, he was sold into slavery in Ireland and sent to tend sheep on Slemish Mountain.

For seven years Patrick looked after his flock before he escaped to France where he preached and taught. But a vision told him that he should return to Ireland. In spite of the opposition of the pagan druids, he preached and taught, bringing Christianity to the Irish people.

Heroes attract myths and legends and there are many legends about St. Patrick. It is said that he stood on a mountaintop and drove all the snakes out of Ireland, and that he is allowed to judge the Irish before they are admitted to heaven!

St. Patrick, patron saint of Ireland, died in 460. He was buried at Dunda-leth-glas, County Down, in the land that he loved.

Q is for Queen Maeve

The Queen of Connacht was Queen Maeve.
No one doubted she was brave.
The great Cuchulainn was brave, too.
Who could have known what he would do?

Queen Maeve of Connacht, also known as Queen Melb, was a warrior, famous for her bravery and her beauty. It was said that enemy soldiers fell down in a swoon at the sight of her and that her own soldiers were all in love with her.

The *Tain*, the great Irish epic, tells of how Queen Maeve went to war to steal a bull. She and her third husband, Ailill, constantly quarreled over which one of them was richer. Ailill insisted he was because he owned a strong, fierce bull. The only better bull, the Brown Bull of Cuailng, was owned by the King and Queen of Ulster. When they refused to sell it to Queen Maeve she went to war to get it. Connacht never did like Ulster, anyway.

Unfortunately for Maeve, the child hero, Cuchulainn, seventeen years old but already known as the "Hound of Ulster," did not swoon at the sight of her or her armies. Instead he drove them back.

Legend says that in spite of the defeat, Queen Maeve got her bull. It was penned up with Ailill's bull and in the end they killed one another, leaving husband and wife just as equal as they had been before.

R is for Riverdance

Dance the jig and dance the reel.
Dance to show the way you feel!
Dance alone or dance in line ...
"Aaragh! Sure you're doing fine!"

Riverdance is the name of a touring Irish dance company that performs worldwide. It started as a six-minute act in 1944 and grew and grew. In traditional Irish dance, the back is straight and the hands are kept pointing down to the sides. In Riverdance the arms and hands move so it is sometimes referred to as "reinvented Irish dancing." The programs change, but they always tell the stories of Ireland. One portrays Irish heroes, one tells of the women of Ireland, and one tells of emigrants and the long goodbye.

Riverdance has brought renewed interest in Irish dancing. But the Irish have always danced. Dancing masters once traveled from village to village giving lessons. They'd meet at fairs and challenge one another to contests that only stopped when one of them collapsed. Good man, the winner!

The shamrock is one of the two national symbols of Ireland (the other is the Irish harp). If you find one you will have good luck for that day, maybe for evermore.

The shamrock's name comes from "seamrog," meaning "little clover." There is not a St. Patrick's parade that doesn't feature it on the banners, on the drums, or clipped to the coats or hats of those who come to cheer. "The wearin' o' the green," it's called. And it's not only the Irish who wear it on St. Paddy's Day either.

Small boxes of cultivated shamrocks are sent from Ireland to loved ones overseas in time for the big day. Even the President of the United States gets a pot from the Irish government.

It's just a little bit of sentiment, a little bit of tradition, and a little bit of home.

S is for Shamrock

Shamrocks growing in the grass,
hard to see them as you pass.
Try to find one. If you do,
Irish luck will come to you.

T is for *Titanic*

The greatest liner ever made.
   "Unsinkable" was what they said.
But she sank slowly out of sight,
   one tragic, starfilled, moonfilled night.

Belfast, Ireland, was one of the most important shipbuilding cities in Europe in the twentieth century. Many of the world's largest ocean liners were built there.

It took two years to build the biggest liner of them all—the RMS *Titanic*. She was 11 stories high and the length of 4 city blocks. Fifteen thousand men worked to complete her. Her watertight compartments made her seem "unsinkable." The pride of Belfast, she was the crown jewel of the Harland and Wolff shipyard.

There were great celebrations at her launching on April 10, 1912. Four days later the *Titanic* collided with an iceberg on her maiden voyage across the Atlantic to New York. She sank on April 14th off the coast of Newfoundland with the loss of more than 1500 lives.

Mr. Thomas Andrews, the *Titanic*'s designer and a managing director of Harland and Wolff's, went down with his ship.

U is for Ulster

Ulster is a province in the North of Ireland.
On its flag it's plain to see a red and bloody hand.
There's trouble still in Ulster. It's very sad to see
Irish fighting Irish in the name of liberty.

Ulster is one of the four provinces of Ireland. It has nine counties, six of which are in Northern Ireland, which is a part of the country still ruled by Britain. Its capital city is Belfast.

Because the people of the Republic of Ireland and some in Ulster want a unified Ireland, Ulster has always been in a state of unrest. In Ireland this dissent is called "the Troubles" and has been responsible for much bloodshed.

The symbol of Ulster is the Red Hand. Legend tells how in the sixteenth century, the Irish hero Hugh O'Neill sailed toward Ulster in a race against other contenders. The High King of Ireland had promised that whoever first laid a hand on Ulster soil would become its King. When close to shore, Hugh O'Neill took his sword, chopped off his right hand, and threw it on to land. There was no doubt who was the winner.

U u

The Vikings of the Northlands were an adventurous, seafaring people with a great desire to explore and conquer other lands. Their average longships were from 66 to 230 feet (20 to 70 meters) long. Called Drakars, they were sailed and rowed by 20 to 30 oarsmen and carried up to 400 warriors. Their sails, often the color of blood, struck fear into the hearts of their enemies. Shields hung from the sides to protect the warriors against spears during sea battles.

For years the Vikings had raided Ireland. But it wasn't until the year 832 that they made their first great attack. They came with a fleet of 120 ships, which held about 10,000 men, landed on Ireland's east coast, and moved inland. They established settlements, mixed with the Irish, and often married Irish women. History says, "not always did the Irish women have a choice."

The Viking era was not entirely a dark night in Ireland. When finally defeated by Brian Boru at the Battle of Clontarf in 1014, they left behind a legacy of shipbuilding and trade with other European countries.

Many stayed in Ireland and became more Irish than the Irish themselves.

V is for Vikings

The Vikings raided Ireland—
they came from far away.
They married Irish women
and decided they would stay!

W is for Writers

There are so many writers
 that it's hard to name them all.
How could they have fitted
 in a country that's so small?

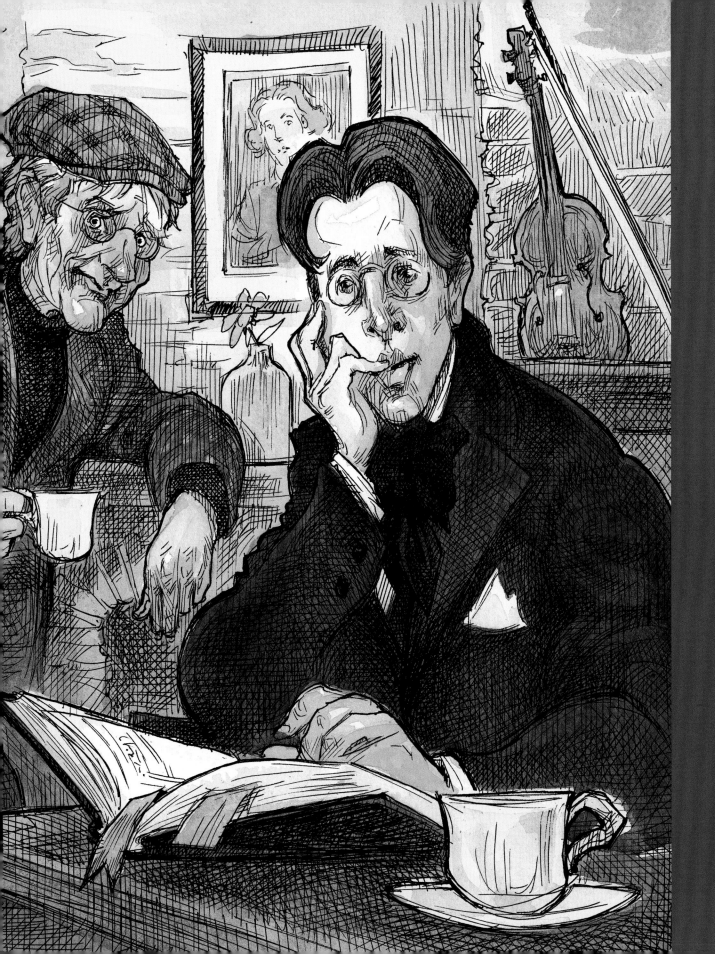

Once upon an olden time in Ireland there were *shanachies*, storytellers who went house to house telling their tales of kings and warriors and heroes of Ireland. They were welcomed in and given a seat by the fire. They were revered.

Many Irish storytellers came after them, writing their stories and poems to share with the people. There was James Joyce, one of the most famous writers of the 1900s, who wrote *Ulysses* and *Finnegan's Wake* and other stories set in Ireland. He himself left the country in dissatisfaction and was buried in Zurich, Switzerland, far from the land that had bred him.

There was W. B. Yeats, the Irish poet perhaps best known for the longing and nostalgia in the poem "The Lake Isle of Innisfree."

There was Edna O'Brien, Sean O'Casey, and others too numerous to list.

Today, Seamus Heaney, the contemporary Irish poet and winner of the Nobel Prize, writes of life in the land that he loves and his pain over the division of Ireland.

Like the shanachies of old, he and the other writers are welcomed in and given a seat by the fire. They are revered.

The letter X does not exist in the Irish alphabet except in math, science, or proper names, nor do the letters J, K, Q, V, W, or Z.

Ireland has two official languages, English and Gaelic, more often called "Irish." Between the seventeenth and twentieth centuries, the Irish language was gradually replaced by English. It is said that the Irish are the only people who took the language of the oppressor and made it sing! Today only a small proportion of the people speak Irish and most of them live on the west coast.

But the native language is in a time of deliberate revival. By order of the national government, names of towns on road signs in the west of Ireland will now have both the English and Irish spellings. For example, Dingle, a favorite tourist town in Southwest Ireland, will be written as Dingle and also as An Daingean (pronounced awn-DANG-in) This way both the English speakers and the Gaelic speakers will be sure to get there. Don't worry though. You can still sing the song "The Dingle Puck Goat" the way you always sang it. If you have a mind to!

X is for X

The Irish alphabet, you'll see,
doesn't use an X or Z.
In Gaelic they're too hard to say,
and so it's easier that way.

Y is for Yarn

When the night is filled with wind and rain
she picks up her needles and works again.
Knit one, slip one, cable three ...
Come home safe from the raging sea.

The pullovers that we call Aran Island sweaters were originally knitted by the island women for their fishermen to wear.

They were made of undyed wool that still held its natural oils. Unique patterns that related to a fisherman's life were knitted into each sweater. There were diamonds like fishing nets, rope stitches, sea waves, and "print of the hoof" patterns that resembled the hoof marks a horse leaves on wet sand. Sometimes the initials or the full name of the wearer was worked into the pattern. If the drowned body of a fisherman washed ashore, he could be identified by the family design on his sweater.

Today Aran Island sweaters are sold all over the world. The name is used for any thick white sweater with a raised pattern. But some of the original heirloom jerseys still survive, museum pieces that speak of a dangerous, seafaring life.